AS YOU FACE THE PHYSICAL, EMOTIONAL, MENTAL CHALLENGES THAT COME WITH A CANCER DIAGNOSIS, THESE AFFIRMATIONS SERVE AS REMINDERS OF THE INCREDIBLE STRENGTH, RESILIENCE, AND COURAGE WITHIN YOU.

THE POWER OF POSITIVITY, HOPE, AND SELF-COMPASSION CAN HAVE A SIGNIFICANT IMPACT ON YOUR WELL-BEING. THE AFFIRMATIONS IN THIS BOOK AIM TO NOURISH YOUR MIND, BODY, AND SPIRIT, PROVIDING ENCOURAGEMENT AND MOTIVATION WHEN YOU NEED IT MOST.

BY EMBRACING THESE AFFIRMATIONS AND INCORPORATING THEM INTO YOUR DAILY LIFE, YOU ARE TAKING AN ACTIVE ROLE IN FOSTERING A POSITIVE MINDSET THAT WILL HELP CARRY YOU THROUGH THIS EXPERIENCE.

WE HOPE THAT THESE 60 POSITIVE AFFIRMATIONS BECOME A VALUABLE COMPANION DURING YOUR JOURNEY, OFFERING ENCOURAGEMENT, INSPIRATION, AND INNER PEACE WHEN YOU NEED IT MOST.

My body is powerful and capable of healing

I am surrounded by love and support from my friends and family

1

I have the strength to overcome any challenge

My determination to fight cancer is unwavering

I choose to focus on positive thoughts and emotions

I am a warrior
and will never
give up

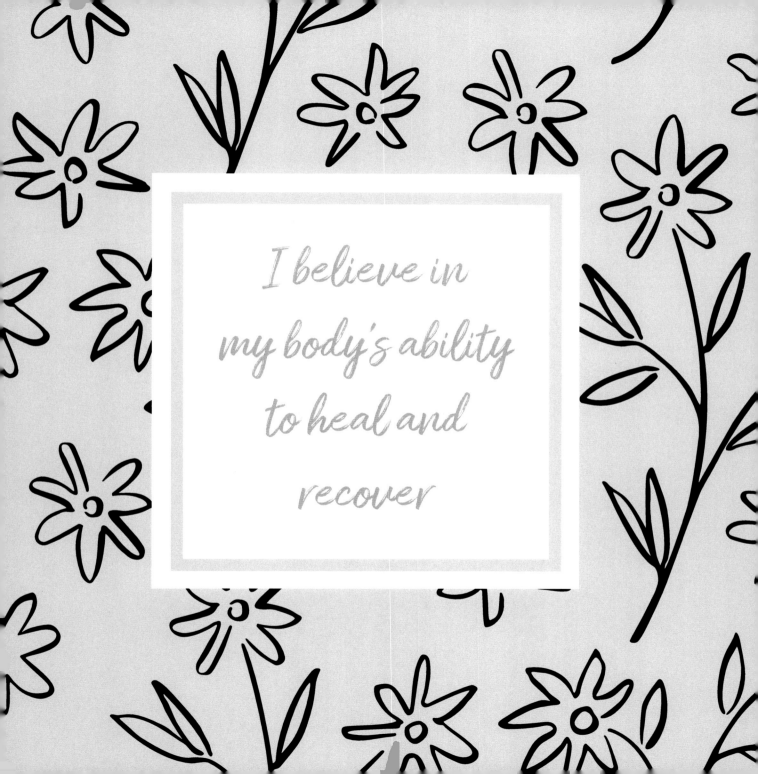

I believe in
my body's ability
to heal and

recover

I am worthy
of a healthy
and happy life

Each day,
I grow stronger
and more
resilient

My spirit is unbreakable and fierce

I celebrate
every victory,
big or small

My positive mindset empowers me to face my fears

I am
committed to my
healing journey

I trust my
medical team
and their
expertise

I am patient and kind to myself during this journey

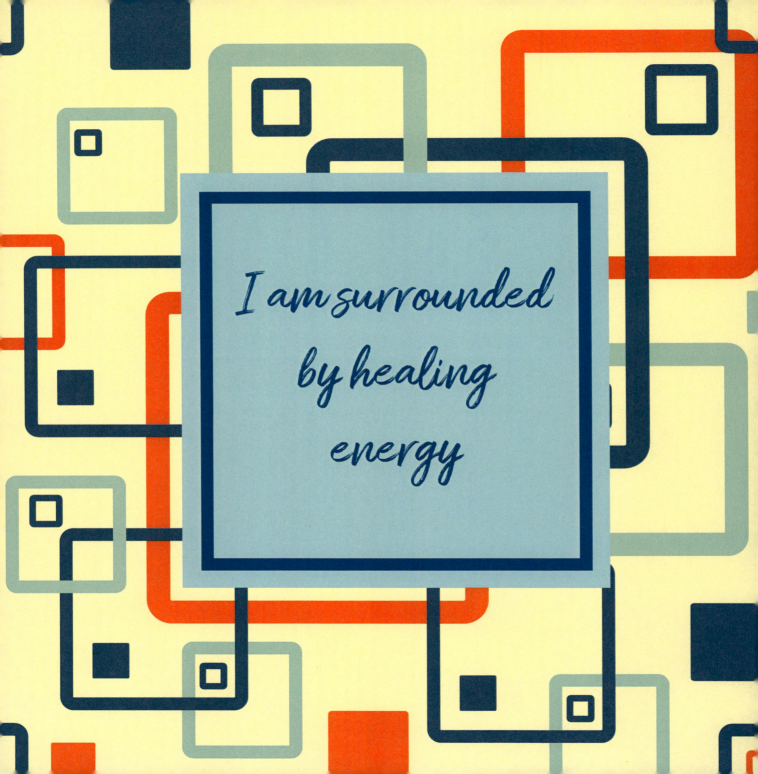

I am surrounded
by healing
energy

I find strength
in vulnerability
and sharing my
story

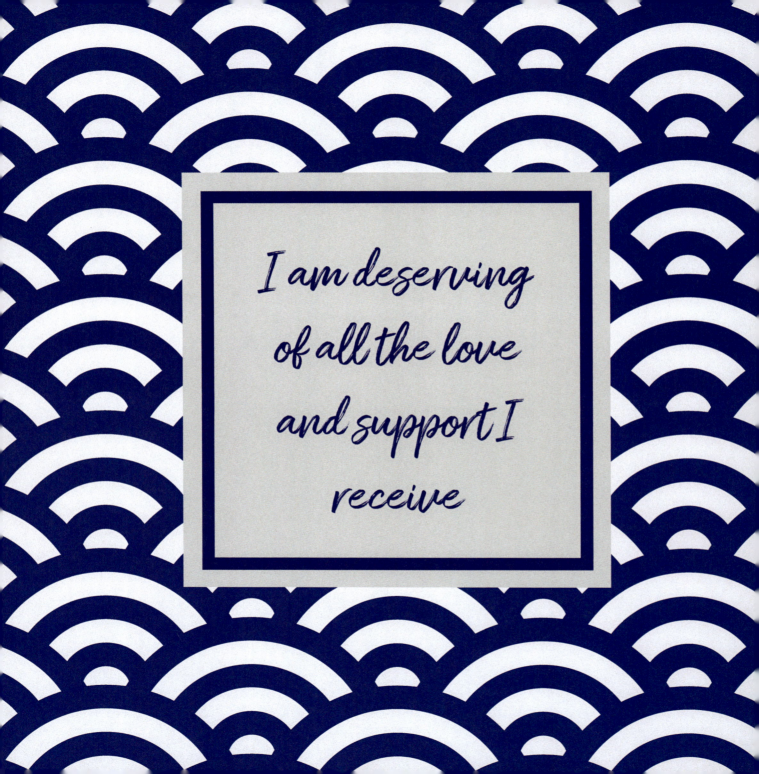

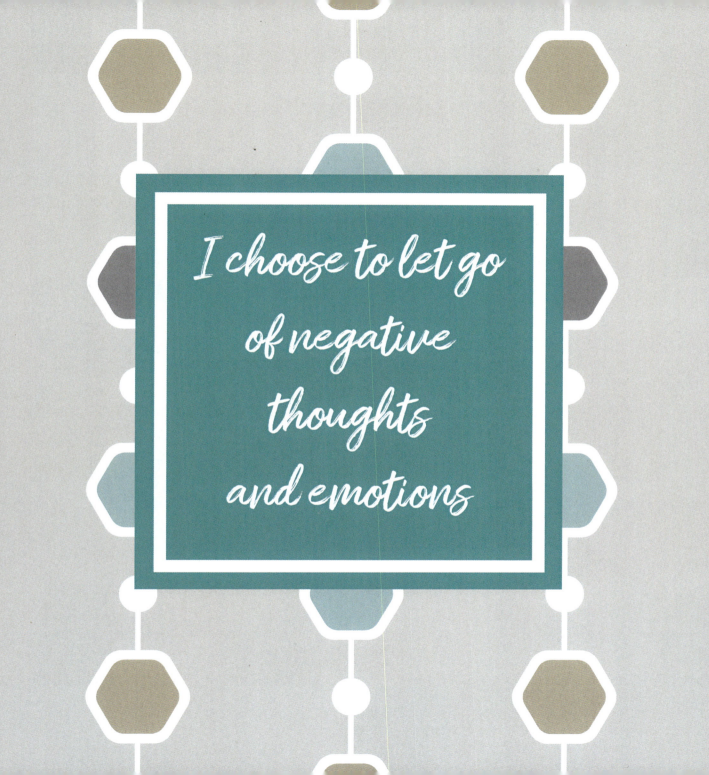

My body is a miraculous vessel capable of healing

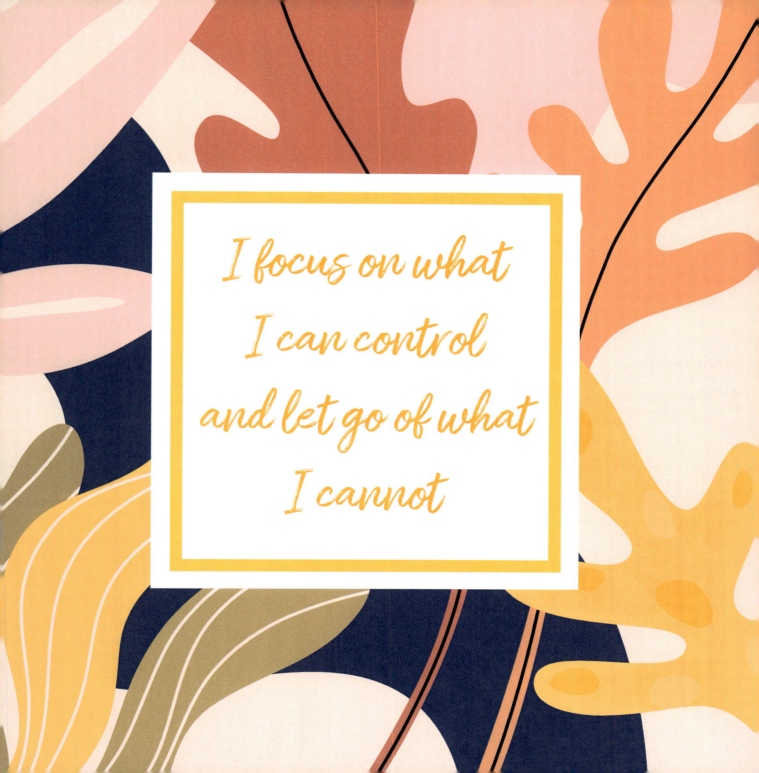

I focus on what
I can control
and let go of what
I cannot

I am dedicated to making healthy choices for my well-being

I prioritize self-care and rest to support my healing

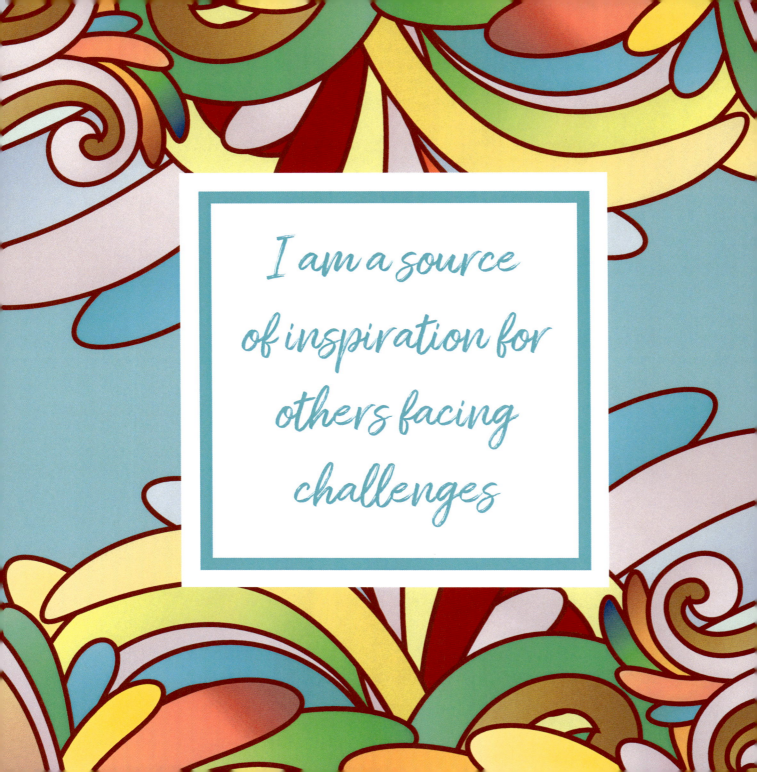

I am a source of inspiration for others facing challenges

My intuition guides me in making the right decisions for my health

I find comfort in knowing I am not alone in this journey

I am a
survivor and
a thriver

I cherish and
appreciate my
body for all
it does for me

I am learning and growing through this experience

I remain hopeful and optimistic about my future

I am grateful
for the strength
and wisdom I've
gained from this

journey

I am surrounded by healing light and positive energy

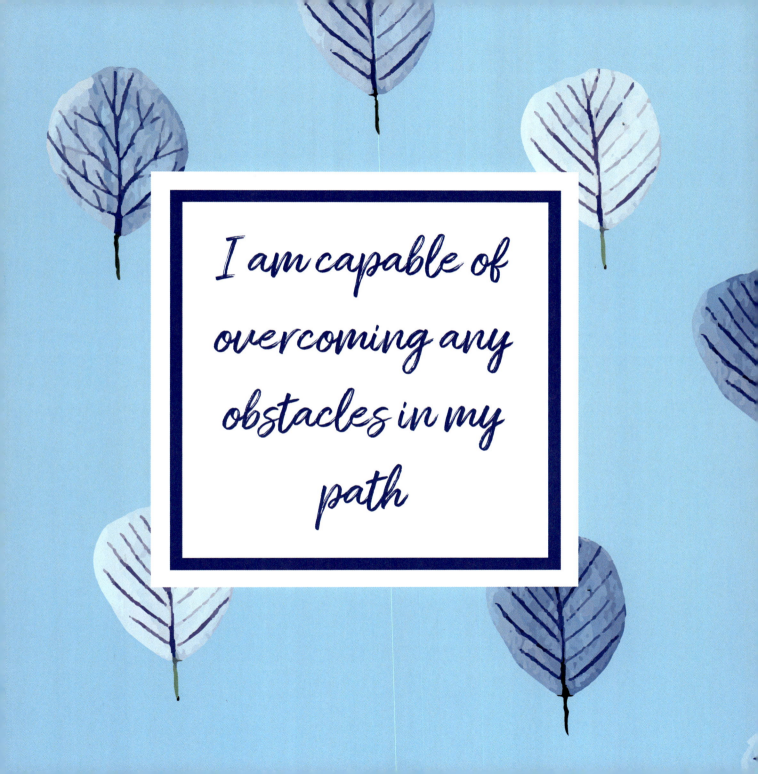

I am capable of overcoming any obstacles in my path

I am proud of
the progress I
have made so far

My body, mind and spirit are working in harmony to heal me

I am grateful
for the love and
care I receive from

my support
network

I am a beacon of hope and strength for myself and others

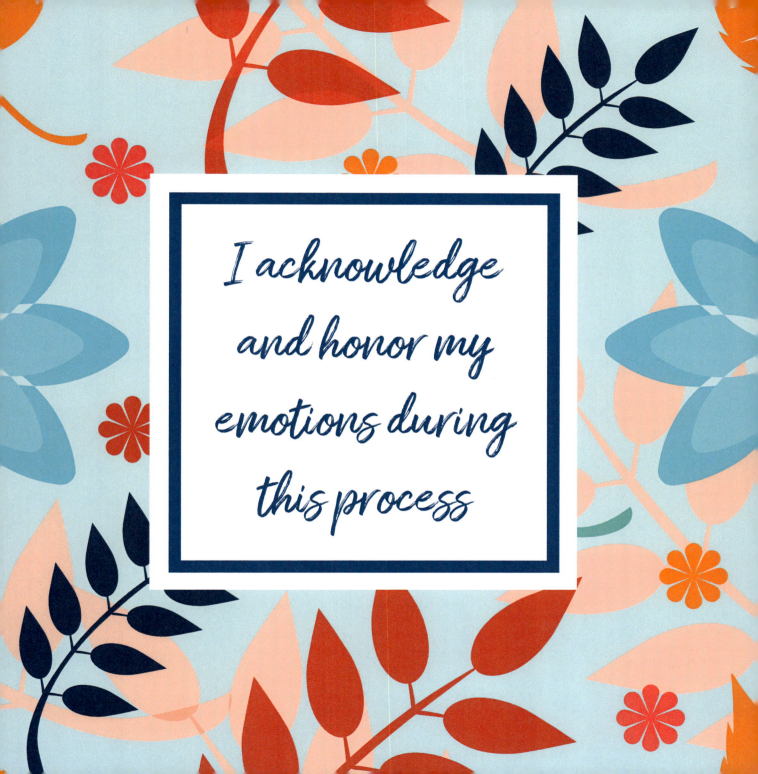

I acknowledge and honor my emotions during this process

I am gentle with myself and embrace self-compassion

I am open to new and innovative treatment options

I trust that the universe is guiding me on my healing journey

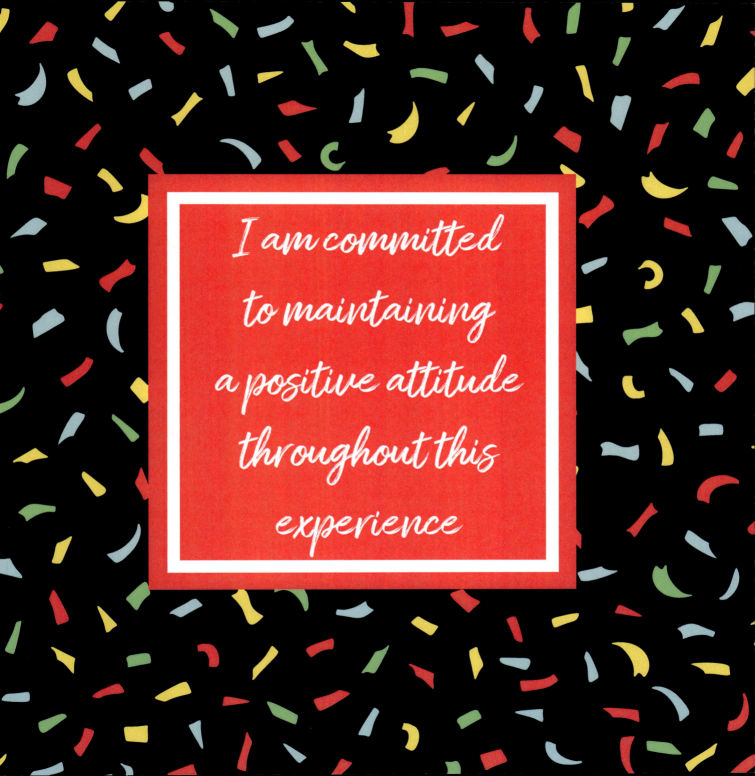

I am committed
to maintaining
a positive attitude
throughout this
experience

I am grateful for the opportunity to grow and transform through this journey

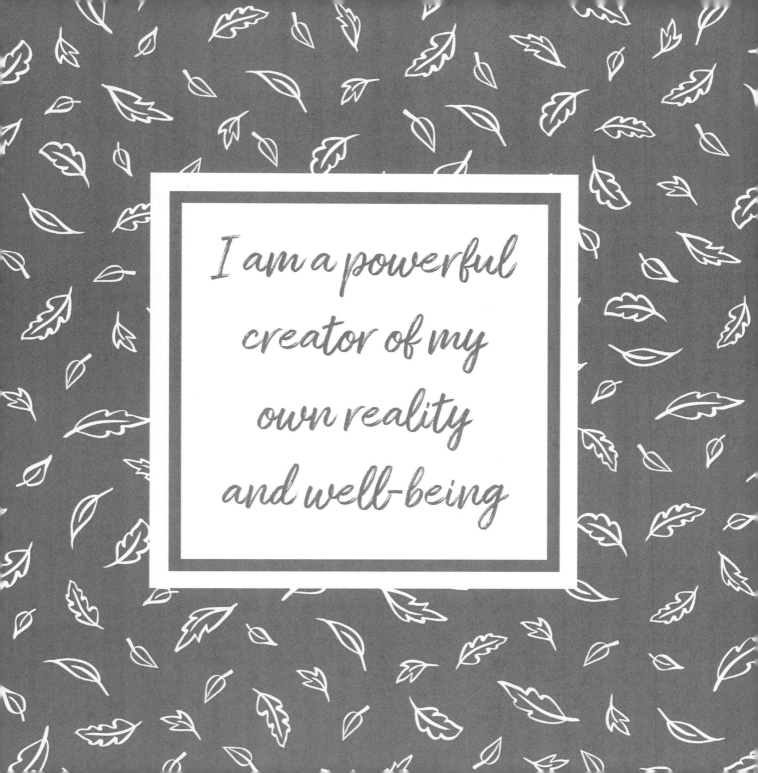

I am a powerful creator of my own reality and well-being

I trust in the power of love and healing energy

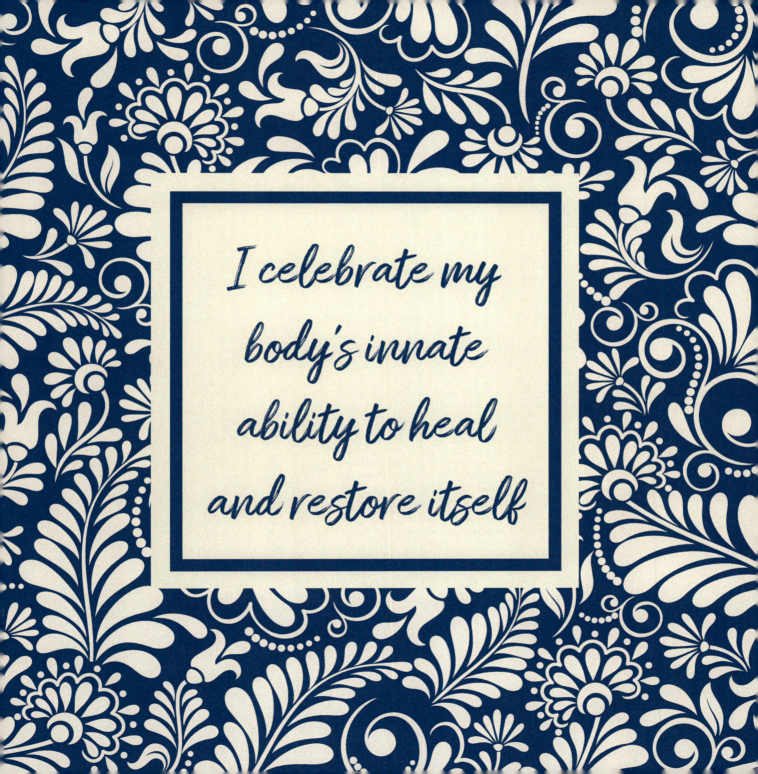

I celebrate my body's innate ability to heal and restore itself

I have faith in my ability to overcome any challenges that come my way

I am surrounded by love and support from my community

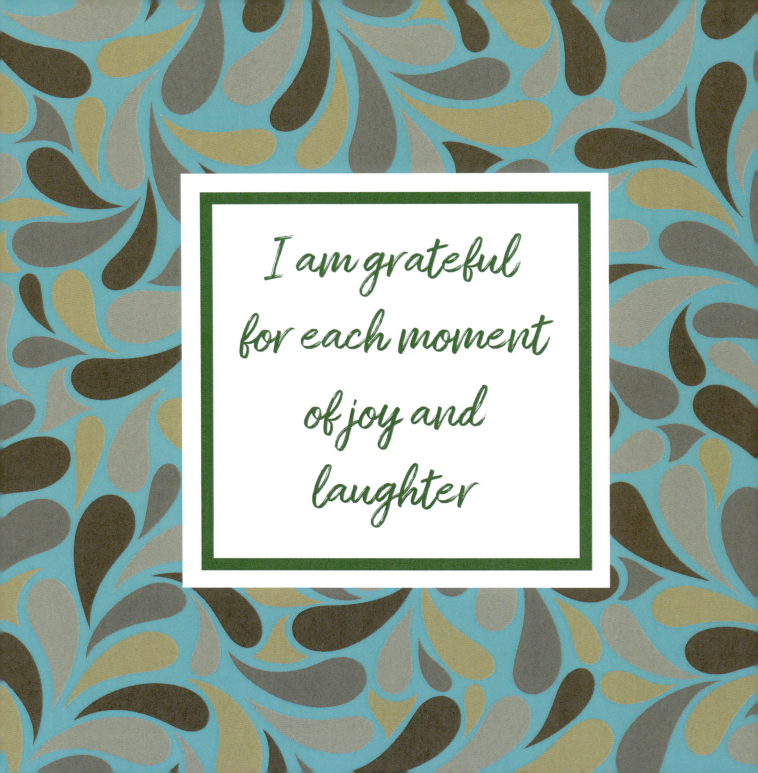

I am grateful
for each moment
of joy and
laughter

I am an unstoppable force in my fight against cancer

I am open to all forms of healing and support

I trust that I am on the right path to healing and recovery.

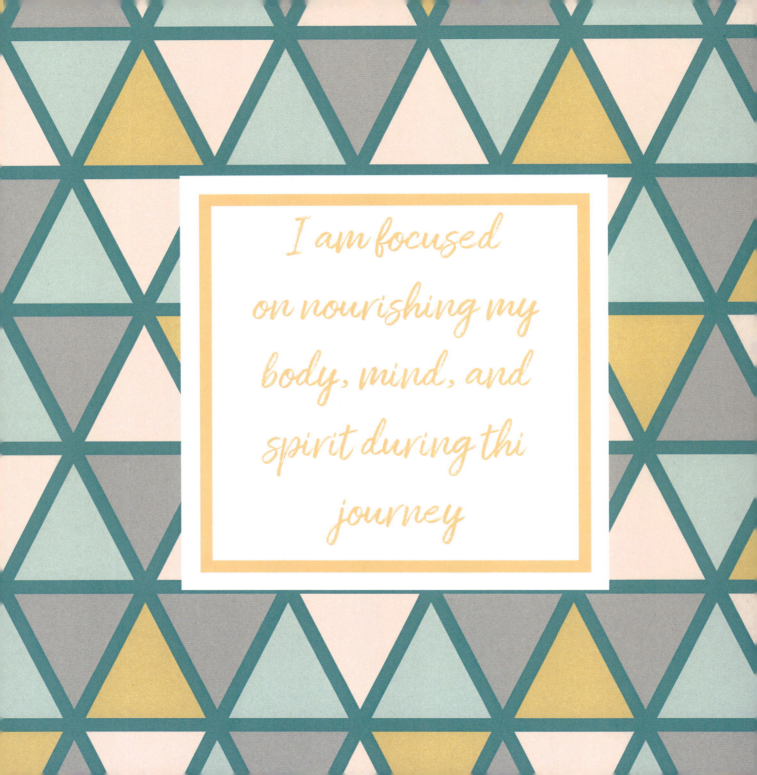

I am focused on nourishing my body, mind, and spirit during thi journey

I am filled with gratitude for the strength and courage I have within me to overcome cancer

I am brave and courageous in my fight against cancer

Made in the USA
Monee, IL
25 May 2025

18124391R00038